# MEXICAN DAY

*Play Three of the trilogy*
*The Ballad of Bimini Baths*

*Tom Jacobson*

**BROADWAY PLAY PUBLISHING INC**
New York
www.broadwayplaypublishing.com
info@broadwayplaypublishing.com

Cover photos by John Perrin Flynn

First edition: August 2018
I S B N: 978-0-88145-792-6

Book design: Marie Donovan
Page make-up: Adobe InDesign
Typeface: Palatino

MEXICAN DAY opened at Rogue Machine Theatre Company (John Perrin Flynn, Producer/Artistic Director; Hollace Starr, Producer; Betsy Zajko, Associate Producer) on 2 June 2018. The cast and creative contributors were:

ZENOBIO REMEDIOS ................................ Jonathan Medina
HISAYE YAMAMOTO .............................................. Jully Lee
BAYARD RUSTIN .................................... Donathan Walters
EVERETT MAXWELL ..................................... Darrell Larson

Director .................................................................... Jeff Liu
Scenic design .................................................. John Iacovelli
Costume design .................................... Dianne K Graebner
Lighting design ..................................................... Brian Gale
Original music/Sound design ............................ Peter Bayne
Stage manager ................................................. Ramón Valdez
Assistant director ............................................ Sam Kofford
Production manager ............................ Amanda Bierbauer
Graphic design .................................... Michelle Hanzelova
Resident technical director .......................... David A Mauer
Casting ...................................................... Victoria Hoffmant

# CHARACTERS & SETTING

HISAYE YAMAMOTO, 26, *a journalist, also plays:*
YASUNARI, *a bath house attendant*
A J MUSTE, *a civil rights leader*
J J WARRICK, *a bath house owner*

BAYARD RUSTIN, 36, *a civil rights activist, also plays:*
NATRICK, *a bath house attendant*
J J WARRICK, *a bath house owner*
YASUNARI, *a bath house attendant*

EVERETT MAXWELL, 64, *an art curator and screenwriter, also plays:*
CARLYLE, *a bath house patron*
TRUDY, *a Southern matron*
OFFICER OLSON, *a policemen*
J J WARRICK, *a bath house owner*

ZENOBIO REMEDIOS, 44, *a bath house attendant, also plays:*
SANTOS, *a bath house attendant*
ALMENA DAVIS, *a newspaper editor*

*The action takes place in and around Bimini Baths and Natural Hot Springs Resort in early 1948.*

*Several locations are depicted primarily through lighting, including an art exhibition in the Los Angeles County Museum of History, Art and Science,* BAYARD'S *hotel room, Bimini Baths (interior and exterior), several night clubs, and the offices of the* Los Angeles Tribune.

# SPECIAL THANKS

Joy Meads, Patricia Garza, Pier Carlo Talenti, Center Theatre Group's L A Writers' Workshop, Son of Semele Ensemble, Lois Arkin, L A Eco Village, Betty Uyeda, John Cahoon, Brent Riggs, Dr William Estrada, Seaver Center for Western History Research, Stan Yogi, Cathy McNassor, Kibo Desoto Knight

# ACT ONE

*(An American soldier, ZENOBIO REMEDIOS, 44, is isolated in light. He stands at attention as a Count Basie song plays [*Taxi War Dance *or* One O'Clock Jump*]. After a few bars, he begins to change out of his Army uniform into a quasi-medical uniform. He has a noticeable limp. The music becomes more distant, and* HISAYE YAMAMOTO, *26, appears isolated in light.)*

HISAYE: *Los Angeles Tribune,* February 25, 1948, Small Talk, by Hisaye Yamamoto. The history of race discrimination in Los Angeles pales in comparison with the peculiar institutions of the American South. But restrictive housing covenants and exclusive public facilities are as common here as lynchings in Mississippi. Discrimination by the ofay segments of the population turns people of all colors against each other. When I was over in Poston, Arizona during the war, I once saw a small Japanese boy taunt a Negro nurse, calling her "kurombo", a word as bad to us as "Jap". It was a punch to my stomach. Now, three years after V J Day, this all-American war is not over, with skirmishes daily in Los Angeles, most recently in the now infamous incident of Bimini Baths.

*(*BAYARD RUSTIN, *36, isolated in light. Clipped accent, almost British)*

BAYARD: Dear Friend A J: Please know that I have the deepest love and respect for you and the other leaders of the Fellowship of Reconciliation. I understand your concern that the target of our Los Angeles integration campaign is a public bathing facility and respect your suggestion that I find a local surrogate so my actions cannot be tainted or perceived as such. I humbly submit that there is no time for alliance-building; I must return to New York shortly. I am, however, familiar with public hygiene establishments, and know how to avoid any appearance of impropriety, conducting myself in a manner that will not violate your trust. I pray that my actions will increase God's power in me and overcome any personal weakness. Love to all, Bayard Rustin.

(EVERETT MAXWELL, *64, isolated in light*)

EVERETT: Fade in: Interior Los Angeles County Museum of History, Science and Art. A marble-walled gallery hung with pastel portraits by Max Wieczorek. Everett Maxwell gazes at the artwork. Still handsome in late middle age, Maxwell is crisply attired, dignified, with an intelligent and thoughtful face, his eyes shadowed by the sadness of a secret.

(ZENOBIO *has almost finished changing clothes.*)

ZENOBIO: February 17, 1948, Bimini Baths and Natural Hot Spring Resort daily log, Admissions Division. Reported by Zenobio Remedios, Assistant Medical Deputy. First day back at Bimini after honorable discharge from the 42nd Rainbow Division of the United States Army. Today's temporary re-assignment to Admissions is due to a telephone inquiry about the Resort's exclusivity policy. It was felt an Army veteran of Spanish background could best respond to any trouble. I am grateful for management's confidence in me as I return to civilian life. Should a problem occur, I'll figure it out. It'll be a piece of cake compared to the Nazis. (*Grins, nervously*)

*(Lights out on all but* BAYARD.*)*

BAYARD: February 17, 1948. Cool and slightly rainy in Los Angeles today, perfect for a relaxing dip— *(Consults a brochure)* —In "a gushing fountain of mineral water with a natural and constant flow of a hundred gallons per minute at a hundred and four degrees Fahrenheit." Bimini Bath complex impressive, a large central building with gables and skylights across the street from the Bimini Inn. Had to take a taxi as streetcar service on the Heliotrope line was abandoned in August. Entered through a portico off Bimini Place and immediately noticed—

*(Lights up on* ZENOBIO *seated at the Admissions desk.* BAYARD *almost does a double take; he finds* ZENOBIO *hot.* ZENOBIO *changes posture, stiffening for the challenge he's been expecting.)*

BAYARD: —A Mexican of rather more than usual attractiveness. This will be either easier or more complicated than expected. *(To* ZENOBIO*)* Good afternoon.

ZENOBIO: Good afternoon, sir.

BAYARD: My name is Bayard Rustin. Yours?

ZENOBIO: Zenobio Remedios. How may I help you, Mr Rustin?

BAYARD: I'd like admission to your plunge, perhaps a therapeutic treatment or two. I'm just visiting Los Angeles, but everyone tells me Bimini is the best in town.

ZENOBIO: I'm sorry, sir. Today is not the day.

BAYARD: Is the plunge not functioning? Are treatments not scheduled? *(Out)* Feigned ignorance of discriminatory practice is the first phase of direct action technique.

ZENOBIO: We're on our regular schedule today, sir.

BAYARD: What treatment do you recommend? *(Consults brochure)* Do you have hot pelvic packs today?

ZENOBIO: We are renowned for our naturally heated treatments, sir.

BAYARD: I see you have a Turkish bath, plain enema—what's the difference between a high enema and a colonic flush?

ZENOBIO: The high enema is more…deeply cleansing.

BAYARD: *(Out)* Say! I believe he flirted with me! *(Reading)* Oh, saline friction with alcoholic rub. I think I accidentally had one of those last night.

ZENOBIO: All our treatments were developed by physicians and thoroughly professional, but—

BAYARD: *(Reading)* Salt rub and manipulations!

ZENOBIO: No treatments are available for you today, Mr Rustin.

BAYARD: *(Indicating brochure)* But it says so right here.

ZENOBIO: If you come back next Thursday—

BAYARD: Next Thursday? I'm here now, you're open—

ZENOBIO: Not…entirely open, sir.

BAYARD: Open, but not open to me.

ZENOBIO: Open to you next Thursday.

BAYARD: *(Out)* Here it comes. *(To* ZENOBIO*)* What's so special about next Thursday?

ZENOBIO: It's Mexican Day.

BAYARD: Isn't Mexican Independence Day in September? And it's not Cinco de Mayo….

ZENOBIO: Mexican Day is when people of Spanish origin may use the plunge.

BAYARD: But I'm not Spanish.

ZENOBIO: Spanish and others.

BAYARD: *(Out)* I will appeal to his sense of solidarity. *(To* ZENOBIO*)* Are you Spanish, Mr Remedios?

ZENOBIO: My father was born in Oaxaca.

BAYARD: So Mexican Day is sort of a celebration of you. Is that when you're allowed to use the pool?

ZENOBIO: Employees are permitted on that day, yes, sir. Please come join us then.

BAYARD: Are there other Spanish employees?

ZENOBIO: A few.

BAYARD: And Negroes? Orientals?

ZENOBIO: I believe so, yes.

BAYARD: All cavorting together in the plunge on Mexican Day. *(Out)* I turned up the heat.

ZENOBIO: We do not cavort. We have behavior standards.

BAYARD: *(Out)* And dropped a hairpin. *(To* ZENOBIO*)* Do you know of any other public bathing facilities in Los Angeles where I might cavort or even frolic without waiting for Spanish Ethiopian Cambodian Day?

ZENOBIO: There are lesser facilities in town, sir, I am sure, but I am not personally familiar with them.

BAYARD: *(Out)* But he knew what I was talking about. I changed tack. *(To* ZENOBIO*)* You were in the war.

ZENOBIO: *(Shifting his leg)* How did you know, Mr Rustin?

BAYARD: Your posture. Straight as a ramrod.

ZENOBIO: Yes, sir. That's how we're trained. Very straight.

BAYARD: *(Out)* Perhaps I was too subtle. *(To* ZENOBIO*)* Navy?

ZENOBIO: Army.

BAYARD: I would have thought Navy. Or at least Marines. Where did you see action?

ZENOBIO: Mr Rustin, I will not be intimidated by your insinuations—

BAYARD: Insinuations?

ZENOBIO: Into permitting you to enter this establishment on a day you are not allowed.

ZENOBIO: You are welcome to return next Thursday— no, not welcome, but unprohibited.

BAYARD: *(Out)* Apparently I touched a nerve. Progress! *(To* ZENOBIO*)* I shall return, but *not* on Mexican Day, the day before the plunge is drained and cleaned, the day of dirtiest water. Now that your establishment's discriminatory policy is clearly articulated—

ZENOBIO: It's perfectly legal—!

BAYARD: I am amazed, Señor Remedios, that you would defend a policy that discriminates against your very self.

ZENOBIO: *(Standing)* Take a powder.

BAYARD: If you call the police, it will only publicize Bimini's fault.

ZENOBIO: I'll throw you out myself!

BAYARD: And which of us do you think would enjoy that more?

*(Lights out on* ZENOBIO.*)*

BAYARD: Perhaps A J is right. I need reinforcements. And relief. Usually one can find some at an art museum.

*(Lights up on* EVERETT *gazing at portraits.* BAYARD *joins him.)*

EVERETT: Iris in, Interior: Gallery. A tall youngish Negro joins Maxwell. They appear absorbed in an image of the head of Christ. *(To* BAYARD *but without looking at him)* There have been many conceptions of the Christ character. A few approach an artistic satisfaction. Very few create a healthy religious atmosphere.

BAYARD: Is this one healthy or unhealthy?

EVERETT: Mr Wieczorek interprets the Man of Sorrows as a vital, yet tender intellectualist of the highest order of his race. A strong, high forehead, firm mouth and determined jaw, sensitive nostrils, and deep, wide-set eyes—eyes that look far—yet deep with sadness and disappointment.

BAYARD: He does look…sensitive.

EVERETT: Close shot: Maxwell gives the Negro a stern look and moves on to the next portrait. The Negro follows.

*(*BAYARD *looks at the portrait, then at* EVERETT, *then back at the portrait again. After one more look at the portrait,* BAYARD *leans forward to read the inscription on the portrait. He turns to* EVERETT.*)*

BAYARD: A privilege to make your acquaintance, Everett C Maxwell.

EVERETT: I'm astonished you can perceive the resemblance. Max drew me decades ago.

BAYARD: He's captured you for all time. Very recognizable, still.

EVERETT: Kind of you to say…?

BAYARD: Bayard Rustin.

EVERETT: They shake hands, warmly.

(BAYARD *and* EVERETT *do.*)

EVERETT: What brings you to the County Museum, Mr Rustin?

BAYARD: I had a rather disappointing day at Bimini Baths and came here in search of—

EVERETT: Rustin gestures toward the portrait.

BAYARD: —Inspiration.

EVERETT: Bimini Baths? Were you able to enter?

BAYARD: I must wait until Mexican Day. Hence my disappointment. What's it like inside?

EVERETT: Oh, I wouldn't know.

BAYARD: You've never been?

EVERETT: Years ago. Around the time of this portrait. I'm sure it's considerably changed since then.

BAYARD: It's been suggested I enlist an ally in storming the Bastille. Is there a Negro newspaper in Los Angeles?

EVERETT: I believe the *Los Angeles Tribune* is run by Negroes.

BAYARD: I will look them up. Is there anywhere else I might refresh myself today?

EVERETT: Refreshment of the spirit, through art. There is also a science wing and a history wing. I was the art curator here once upon a time.

BAYARD: I've only just arrived from New York. My body is in need of refreshment even more than my spirit.

EVERETT: Maxwell gives Rustin a stern look. They move back to the Head of Christ. (*To* BAYARD) This Christ sees humanity centuries ahead. What a tragic vision to a man whose one desire was to leave with us the secret of redemption. Are you a religious man, Mr Rustin? Do you believe in redemption? *(Out)* To Maxwell's astonishment, the Negro begins to sing, full throttle, in the middle of the art gallery.

BAYARD: *(Sings) En una noche oscura* [On a dark night]

EVERETT: His voice is a rich tenor, beautiful in tone and timbre. *(To* BAYARD*)* That's—that's—! I recognize it—

BAYARD: *Con ansias en amores inflamada* [Fevered with love in love's anxiety]

EVERETT: It's sixteenth century! *The Dark Night of the Soul* by Saint John of the Cross!

BAYARD: *Oh dichosa ventura!* [O hapless-happy plight!]

EVERETT: Maxwell joins in the song, his voice a mellow baritone.

BAYARD & EVERETT:
*Sali sin ser notada* [I went, none seeing me]
*Estando ya mi casa sosegada* [Forth from my house where all things be]

*(Lights out on* BAYARD *and* EVERETT *and up on* HISAYE.*)*

HISAYE: Dear reader, my own involvement in the Bimini incident began awkwardly, almost against my will, a premonition of what was to come. I was proofing an article on the restrictive covenants of Compton, when—

*(*BAYARD *joins* HISAYE, *looks puzzled, steps out, then comes back in.)*

BAYARD: Are these the offices of the *Los Angeles Tribune*?

HISAYE: A Model of Journalism.

BAYARD: Pardon?

HISAYE: Our motto.

BAYARD: I was told the *Tribune* was a Negro paper—

HISAYE: Hisaye Yamamoto, Nisei Correspondent.

(BAYARD *and* HISAYE *shake hands.*)

BAYARD: Bayard Rustin—

HISAYE: Oh, Mr Rustin, pardon me! I didn't mean to be flippant. Some of us are great admirers of your work with the Fellowship of Reconciliation—I covered your speech to the Japanese American Citizen's League—

BAYARD: Thank you, Miss Yamamoto—

HISAYE: Please call me Si. How can I help? Are you in Los Angeles to organize...anything?

BAYARD: Possibly. Is there someone...?

HISAYE: Someone Negro?

BAYARD: Well...someone in charge?

HISAYE: Someone male?

BAYARD: The editor—

HISAYE: Almena Davis. She's not male, but she is Negro. Unfortunately, Almena's out this afternoon. So is everyone else. For the moment, I am the foremost Negro newspaper in the West.

BAYARD: Could you let Miss Davis know I'm inquiring about a newspaper campaign against discrimination at Bimini Baths?

HISAYE: I wouldn't wait for Almena if I were you. She wasn't exactly fanatical about Mr Gandhi.

BAYARD: If you take no action, nothing changes.

HISAYE: The paper does its part by simply reporting the truth.

BAYARD: To Negroes.

HISAYE: We are...advised not to become the story, not get too involved. Last year a Negro man named

Short came to us after his family moved into a white neighborhood in Fontana. Nasty words scrawled on their house, broken windows—

BAYARD: How did the paper help?

HISAYE: Not even an article until too late. A few weeks later there was an arson fire. The whole family…

BAYARD: I'm sorry. That must be very frustrating.

HISAYE: We're a Negro paper and we let a Negro family die in order to maintain—what? —Our journalistic integrity?

BAYARD: There are many kinds of integrity.

HISAYE: So I'm sorry, but you won't find official support for your newspaper campaign here.

BAYARD: Perhaps there's someone at the paper who might feel morally bound—?

HISAYE: Me.

BAYARD: But I'm looking for—

HISAYE: I've always been curious what Bimini Baths looks like inside. My white friends tell me it's killer diller.

BAYARD: Direct action? You'd be disobeying the newspaper's policy.

HISAYE: I'm tired of obeying.

BAYARD: Miss Yamamoto—

HISAYE: Si. You really should call me Si if we're going to be disobedient together.

*(Lights out on them and up on* ZENOBIO.*)*

ZENOBIO: February 18, 1948. Admissions log, Zenobio Remedios reporting. Many requests for the Thermo Therapeutic Oven due to the cool weather, but nothing unusual until—

(HISAYE *approaches* ZENOBIO.)

HISAYE: Good evening.

ZENOBIO: Miss.

HISAYE: What are your rates?

ZENOBIO: Here's our brochure, Miss. Everything on this side is available a week from tomorrow.

HISAYE: I'd like a treatment today.

ZENOBIO: I'm sorry, Miss, but Bimini Hot Spring and Resort is an exclusive establishment.

HISAYE: I only want the best.

ZENOBIO: Then we look forward to welcoming you next week.

HISAYE: I want the best today.

ZENOBIO: Look, Miss, don't play dumb.

HISAYE: Pardon me, Mister—?

ZENOBIO: You know I can't let you in today. Please don't make a stink.

HISAYE: I'm here to cleanse myself of any stink, Mister—?

ZENOBIO: Remedios. Zenobio Remedios. Ask for me by name and I'll give you a discount…if you come back next Thursday.

HISAYE: I should hope I'd get a discount with the water so dirty.

ZENOBIO: Our one hundred percent naturally heated spring water is—

HISAYE: Filthy at the end of the month and full of Mexicans.

(ZENOBIO *just stares at* HISAYE, *astonished.*)

HISAYE: Isn't it? On Mexican Day?

ZENOBIO: I've been perfectly polite with you, Miss—

HISAYE: Hisaye Yamamoto. But you can call me Si because we're going to become very good friends.

ZENOBIO: No, Miss, I don't think—

HISAYE: I will be ubiquitous until you admit me.

ZENOBIO: Thursday next.

HISAYE: I'll just settle into your vestibule and we can chat. Every day. For hours.

ZENOBIO: Miss Yamamoto—

HISAYE: Si!

ZENOBIO: I'm sorry, protocol requires us to address our patrons by last name.

HISAYE: Well, that's progress. At least now I'm a patron.

ZENOBIO & HISAYE: Thursday next.

HISAYE: Mr Remedios—

ZENOBIO: Zeno.

HISAYE: I was abiding by your sacred protocol, Mr Remedios.

ZENOBIO: Staff may be addressed by first name.

HISAYE: Very well, Zeno. What time does your shift end?

ZENOBIO: You'll have no better luck with the fellow on the next shift.

HISAYE: Oh, for seven hakes! I'm asking if you'd like to meet me after work for an unofficial discussion.

ZENOBIO: You mean…a date? You're asking me out on a date?

HISAYE: Of course not a date.

ZENOBIO: I can't take you on a date!

HISAYE: But away from your place of employment—

ZENOBIO: It's against policy for employees to—

HISAYE: —You could drop that white mask you're wearing and tell me what it's like to work where you're not permitted to play!

BAYARD: *(Appearing)* Miss, is this man annoying you?

ZENOBIO: You again!

HISAYE: A little bit. Zeno is very stubborn—

ZENOBIO: I know what this is—!

HISAYE: —That's his nickname, by the way—he said I can call him Zeno—

ZENOBIO: This is deliberate—!

BAYARD: This young lady would like to enter your establishment—

ZENOBIO: You're double-teaming me!

HISAYE: And he's asked me out on a date.

BAYARD: A date! He can't do that!

ZENOBIO: I have not!

BAYARD: You're my date!

ZENOBIO: No, I can't!

BAYARD: Get your paws off my girl!

ZENOBIO: What?

HISAYE: After he gets off work tonight.

ZENOBIO: That's not so!

BAYARD: I'll show him!

ZENOBIO: She asked me! And I said no!

(BAYARD *grabs* HISAYE *and kisses her. She seems surprised for half a moment, but then returns the kiss.* ZENOBIO *stares, confused. Lights out on* BAYARD *and* HISAYE.)

ZENOBIO: Swell! How do I put *that* in a report?

*(Lights out on* ZENOBIO *and up on* BAYARD.*)*

BAYARD: Si and I reconnoitered back at the Tribune.

*(Lights up on* HISAYE.*)*

HISAYE: I presume you're Uranian.

BAYARD: *(Laughs)* Uranian!?

HISAYE: I was trying to find a polite word.

BAYARD: There is no polite word.

HISAYE: Homosexual?

*(*BAYARD *gestures "of course".)*

HISAYE: Poor Zeno! He must be so confused.

BAYARD: If he's a jealous man, one or the other of us is about to get that date.

HISAYE: He's a little old for me.

BAYARD: But handsome, yes?

*(*HISAYE *shrugs, "yes, he's handsome".)*

HISAYE: This is the most radical direct action ever. I'm familiar with sit-ins, but whoever heard of a kiss-in before?

BAYARD: You weren't making any genuine progress, so I improvised.

HISAYE: So much for not being the story. Almena would kill me.

BAYARD: Put it in your column! Imagine a hundred Negroes and Japanese camped out in front of Bimini Baths—

HISAYE: Kissing!

BAYARD: And don't be vain—you're not the story.

HISAYE: *You* are? Talk about vain!

BAYARD: Zeno is.

HISAYE: He didn't tell you to call him Zeno.

BAYARD: He will.

HISAYE: Why's he the story?

BAYARD: He's a Mexican forced to defend racist policy in order to keep his job. He's a vet! Who hasn't come home to a hero's welcome but to be a house nigger.

HISAYE: Please don't use that ugly word. It revolts my stomach.

BAYARD: That's why I used it. You can write his story, break everyone's heart, like yours was broken by that fire in Fontana. Redeem yourself.

HISAYE: I can't write from his point of view, especially without his permission, which he would never grant.

BAYARD: Why not?

HISAYE: I'm a Japanese woman, not a Mexican man.

BAYARD: You'll see through his eyes, understand him better.

HISAYE: You're amusingly idealistic.

BAYARD: And the better you know him, the easier it will be to write from his point of view. *(Winks)*

HISAYE: Wow! Did you just wink at me? Stop winking at me!

*(Lights out on* BAYARD *and* HISAYE *and up on* ZENOBIO.*)*

ZENOBIO: In order to outflank Miss Yamamoto by preventing her threatened occupation of our vestibule, I agreed to meet her for a drink at Shepp's Playhouse in Little Tokyo.

*(Music. Lights up on* HISAYE *in the middle of an awesome Bette Davis impression.)*

HISAYE: Every time you kiss me, I have to wipe my mouth! Wipe my mouth!

(ZENOBIO *laughs.*)

HISAYE: What's *your* favorite movie?

ZENOBIO: I like Westerns.

HISAYE: Such as?

ZENOBIO: *The Old Code, The Eyes of the Totem.*

HISAYE: Those are twenty years old. Anything recent?

ZENOBIO: They're very well written.

HISAYE: This is Hollywood. The writer's not important.

ZENOBIO: Nothing is real until written.

HISAYE: How long have you been working at Bimini?

ZENOBIO: I just started back after my discharge, but altogether almost ten years.

HISAYE: Is it fulfilling work?

ZENOBIO: It's not perfect, but kind of a home. It's where I learned to swim when I was a kid. I got a lotta history.

HISAYE: Guarding the door against colored people?

ZENOBIO: Normally I work in medical, doing treatments.

HISAYE: But is that what you want to do with your life?

ZENOBIO: Is this a job interview?

HISAYE: Just a drink.

ZENOBIO: Before the war I was saving up for college. I wanted to study paleontology at Yale.

HISAYE: Do you still?

ZENOBIO: I'm forty-four years old.

HISAYE: G I Bill.

ZENOBIO: You go to college?

HISAYE: Compton Junior College. Why paleontology?

ZENOBIO: I cleaned fossils from the Tar Pits when I was thirteen. *(Produces a small brown bone)*

HISAYE: Is that a fossil?

ZENOBIO: It's a dire wolf baculum.

HISAYE: What's a baculum?

ZENOBIO: A…uh…penis bone.

HISAYE: Well.

ZENOBIO: Sorry. *(Puts bone away)*

HISAYE: Did you use gasoline?

ZENOBIO: Kerosene.

HISAYE: We lived in an oil field for a while and my brother Jemo fell in a sump hole when he was three. My parents siphoned gas from the car to clean the tar baby off.

ZENOBIO: I cleaned a guy like that once at Bimini.

HISAYE: A grown man?

ZENOBIO: He got drunk and fell in La Brea, stained so dark no white hospital would take him. This crazy Negro named Amen helped me turn a white man white again!

HISAYE: I never heard about that! When was it?

ZENOBIO: 1939. Soon after, Amen died in the Port Chicago explosion. He might not've gotten drafted so fast if he listened to me and kept his head down.

HISAYE: How sad. Were you friendly?

ZENOBIO: Okay friendly. He was a funny guy.

HISAYE: But what an intriguing story! Have you written it down?

ZENOBIO: I'm still figuring it all out.

HISAYE: Aren't we all?

ZENOBIO: The tar, the war. I'm trying to apply science.

HISAYE: To the human condition?

ZENOBIO: Hate. Love. There's even math in there somewhere. *(Pause)* Who's that Negro came with you to Bimini? Your boyfriend?

HISAYE: Mr Rustin is very famous. He went to prison as a conscientious objector. He agitates.

ZENOBIO: I can see that. But is he your boyfriend?

HISAYE: My, you're insistent. Now you're interviewing me.

ZENOBIO: Never mind. None of my beeswax.

HISAYE: Why do you want to know?

ZENOBIO: He kiss you like that in public all the time?

HISAYE: I don't believe I'm ready to answer that quite yet. Maybe after another drink.

*(Lights out on* HISAYE *and* ZENOBIO *and up on* EVERETT *and* BAYARD, *also having a drink.)*

EVERETT: Interior: Bar. The Finale Club is one of those fly-by-night establishments of Bronzeville, closing every few weeks and opening up somewhere slightly less posh. A place where a Negro and a Caucasian can drink in peace. Rustin may have had a bit too much sauce. Maxwell maintains his dignity.

BAYARD: Why not?

EVERETT: It's not my fight. I don't fight. I observe.

BAYARD: It is too your fight.

EVERETT: *(Out)* Maxwell is irritated. *(To* BAYARD*)* In case you haven't noticed, Mr Rustin, I'm a white man.

BAYARD: Still handsome in late middle age.

EVERETT: Thank you, but—

BAYARD: I'm vividly aware of your whiteness. It's extreme. You may be the whitest man I ever met.

EVERETT: White people are your dilemma, isn't that so?

BAYARD: Not the people—

EVERETT: The Negro is not the dilemma.

BAYARD: I agree—it's the white man's burden.

EVERETT: *(Out)* Maxwell ignores that remark. *(To* BAYARD*)* You mustn't expect Caucasians to solve the dilemma. The Negro must come up with the solution. You're motivated.

BAYARD: We can't do it alone.

EVERETT: Nor can you sit around waiting for white people—

BAYARD: I don't sit around. Occasionally I loiter, but with intent.

EVERETT: *(Out)* Maxwell ignores that remark, too.

BAYARD: The problem will not be solved until *everybody* does what they can do.

EVERETT: They say Bimini's not what it used to be. A bit run down.

BAYARD: Come see for yourself.

EVERETT: I'm not reluctant. Nor stubborn. I admire your ambition. I simply cannot go into Bimini Baths.

BAYARD: Yes, you can. Any day of the week.

EVERETT: Mr Rustin, we are only recently acquainted, so I'm not comfortable giving you the details, but I'm banned from Bimini.

BAYARD: Banned?

EVERETT: For life.

BAYARD: What did you do?

EVERETT: An indiscretion—

BAYARD: I've been arrested more times than I can count—

EVERETT: A serious indiscretion.

BAYARD: How long ago?

EVERETT: Nineteen sixteen.

BAYARD: Whatever you did—and I won't insist you tell me, despite my immense curiosity—you did it thirty-two years ago! The staff of Bimini, the attendants, the dashing wounded Mexican veteran barring the door won't remember your sin—he would have been a child at the time.

EVERETT: I was drummed out of society, not just Bimini Baths. Dismissed from the Museum. My humiliation was quite public.

BAYARD: But you can't tell me.

EVERETT: Let's not taint our fresh acquaintance with too much truth.

BAYARD: *(Out)* Mr Maxwell appears to be one of those. Self-loathing. *(To* EVERETT*)* I respect your privacy and withdraw my request.

EVERETT: For thirty-two years I've cautiously crabwalked back into the world, behind pen names, pseudonyms, daring after ten years to sign my initials, only after twenty my full name! My more steadfast friends did their best for me—Max Wieczorek was thoughtful, generous, invited me to write the preface to his *catalogue raisonne*. But many turned their backs. You have no idea what it's like to be so ostracized—

*(*BAYARD *just stares at* EVERETT*.)*

EVERETT: Well. Yes, you do. I apologize. But. I can't. You understand.

BAYARD: Of course.

EVERETT: *(Out)* Medium shot. They sit in silence. Each contemplating his sins.

BAYARD: *(Out)* I realize he's a different generation—

EVERETT: *(Out)* Close-up: Rustin.

BAYARD: *(Out)* —Grew up in a different world—

EVERETT: *(Out)* His noble dark face focused inward, his calm eyes half-lidded as he wonders whether he could have done what Maxwell has done, what he imagines Maxwell's hideous transgression to be.

BAYARD: *(Out)* —A sensibility forged before he War to End All Wars, this Edwardian innocence, his privileged prudishness gassed in Flanders fields. He knows what is right, but fears himself.

EVERETT: *(Out)* Close-up: Maxwell.

EVERETT: He flushes to the roots of his hair, embarrassed to have revealed so little yet said too much. His shame buried in newspaper archives and sealed court records, in prison rolls and pleading letters, in cold parole reports.

BAYARD: I realize I must live in the present, or better yet the future. have to imagine what I can be, not what is. The Second World War cracked everything open, destroyed so much, and now we can go back to a better time, way back—

EVERETT: But maybe—

BAYARD: A better time that—

BAYARD & EVERETT: No one remembers!

EVERETT: And isn't that worse?

*(Lights out on* BAYARD *and* EVERETT *and up on* HISAYE *and* ZENOBIO. *From their posture, it's clear they've had that second drink.)*

ZENOBIO: I maintained good control of the Yamamoto situation until we'd almost finished the second round.

HISAYE: Everyone in Poston went a little mad. Freud would have had a field day with us! Respectable people coping with the unpredictable, the unimaginable. Some of us better than others.

ZENOBIO: You seem okay.

HISAYE: Trust me, I'm not. Just wait. I'm becoming a very disobedient girl. I could end up like Miss Sakiyama.

ZENOBIO: What happened to her?

HISAYE: She had delicate sensibilities, the camp turned her, or maybe just revealed her, her madness, when the rest of us kept it hidden.

ZENOBIO: What'd she do?

HISAYE: She got khaki wacky. One of the boys woke up in the middle of the night to find her sitting at the foot of his bed watching him. Yum, yum, eat 'em up. Everybody talked about her. It was quite shocking to me as a proper young girl. Could that happen to me one day?

ZENOBIO: Maybe she was always like that, like you said.

HISAYE: Possibly, but the concentration camp brought it out.

ZENOBIO: Concentration camp? We didn't have those here!

HISAYE: Internment camp, concentration camp, what's the difference?

ZENOBIO: We're not Nazis! You weren't starved, gassed, shoved in ovens!

HISAYE: No, the war ended. But what if?

ZENOBIO: Not the same thing.

HISAYE: You weren't there.

ZENOBIO: You weren't at Dachau.

HISAYE: You were?

ZENOBIO: We liberated the camp.

HISAYE: So you're a hero.

ZENOBIO: Hardly.

HISAYE: Which division?

ZENOBIO: Forty-second Rainbow. Don't believe me, do you?

HISAYE: There were Mexican units in Europe—?

ZENOBIO: We were classified white—

HISAYE: My brother was in a Nisei unit—

ZENOBIO: The 522nd Field Artillery Battalion? They were the only Japanese near Dachau—

HISAYE: No, he was—          ZENOBIO: —At Kaufering
                                                                and Landsberg—

ZENOBIO: So your brother didn't see Dachau—

HISAYE: No, he didn't—

ZENOBIO: Didn't smell it!

HISAYE: You're right, he          ZENOBIO: Didn't get it
was in Italy—                              under his skin!

ZENOBIO: Before we got there, the officers warned us not to go near the prisoners—

HISAYE: I know it was a          ZENOBIO: —Lice, diseases—
bad business—                            but no one told the
                                                        prisoners.

ZENOBIO: When they saw us they swarmed, hugging us with their dirty, bony arms, sweeping us into their joy, their disbelief at being saved. Then one leftover SS tried to escape, made a break for the ditch by the fence.

*(Surreptitiously,* HISAYE *scribbles in an old but elegant leather-bound notebook.)*

ZENOBIO: The prisoners made a horrible sound, a groan, a hiss—and chased the German guard, taking us with them, making us part of their filthy mob. The S S bastard almost made it, but slipped and fell in the ditch, a moat, really, some water but not very deep. The prisoners followed, piled in on top of him in the ditch, dragging me along, and stood on him, holding him down with our collective weight. You could hear his screams at first, but couldn't see him. He shut up when someone stood his head, holding it under the muddy water. Maybe it was me. All I could think was that Kraut under my boots had documented or dumped the decaying human meat we saw all over the camp. Madder than your Miss Sacajawea, I stood my ground till I couldn't feel him moving, till I was as wet and filthy as the prisoners, as guilty as the S S man, till there *was* no S S man.

*(*HISAYE *starts crying.)*

ZENOBIO: I never got court-martialed, chewed out in any way. But my boots didn't protect me. When I crushed him under the water, something broke in my foot, too. Never been the same. But at the time I didn't feel it at all.

HISAYE: That's…a terrible story. You must feel—

ZENOBIO: Like I was covered with tar. No way to get clean.

HISAYE: I'm sorry—I— *(She pulls herself together.)*

ZENOBIO: So, no, I'm not a hero…like your brother.

HISAYE: He wasn't—

ZENOBIO: We saw different things: me, you, your brother.

HISAYE: My brother didn't see what you saw cause he never saw 1945. He was killed in Italy in 1944.

ZENOBIO: Condolences.

HISAYE: Johnny was my favorite.

ZENOBIO: He did what he had to, like all of us.

HISAYE: He didn't have to! Johnny died for the country that imprisoned his family. You're defending a policy that imprisons you.

ZENOBIO: Aw, we were having a nice time!

HISAYE: I know you're just back from Europe and all—

ZENOBIO: Weren't we having a nice time? Getting along?

HISAYE: But it's different here now. We're a different country from before.

ZENOBIO: We're a country where a Japanese girl— *(Snatches her notebook)* —Writes for a colored paper. *(Out)* I'd made inquiries.

HISAYE: I have that privilege, yes.

ZENOBIO: You didn't tell me. *(He flips through her notebook.)*

HISAYE: The paper doesn't even support—it's Bayard who wants me to write about it, be the civil rights Lois Lane—!

ZENOBIO: You talk about me with him?

HISAYE: You and I talk about him.

ZENOBIO: You never did say if he was your boyfriend.

HISAYE: He's not. It is in fact none of your beeswax, but he's definitely not.

(ZENOBIO *just looks at* HISAYE.)

HISAYE: He's queer! And I know for a fact he'd have no objection to me telling you.

ZENOBIO: I don't care about that.

HISAYE: And yet you interrogate me about him.

ZENOBIO: The interrogation's mutual, ain't it?

HISAYE: I'm just doing—

ZENOBIO: Your job.

HISAYE: My moral duty.

ZENOBIO: So I'm the means to an end? A good story?

HISAYE: No! Not just—you're many things—more than I thought: a vet, a paleontologist, a man with a penis bone and guilty—foot—

ZENOBIO: And all that's going into your column? *Small Talk*? Everything I just told you? All that crummy personal—shit—?

HISAYE: If I write it, I'll write from your point of view—

ZENOBIO: This hits the paper, even a colored paper, I'll lose my job—

HISAYE: Maybe you should! It's a lackey job! What they're making you do is immoral.

ZENOBIO: It's my lackey job! You got no right to my morals. No right to my story, Rois Rane!

HISAYE: (*After a moment*) I see why you're classified white.

ZENOBIO: You're a cold-blooded little number.

HISAYE: But they can't help talking like that. They're white.

ZENOBIO: You're not me. (*Throws notebook at her*) You can't write—me.

HISAYE: I'm a young Japanese woman. Does that mean I can't write about anybody old? About men? Mexicans? May I only write about myself?!

*(Lights out on* HISAYE.*)*

ZENOBIO: It was not easy. But I did. My job.

*(Lights out on* ZENOBIO *and up on* BAYARD.*)*

BAYARD: *(Out)* Dear Friend A J: I have followed your advice and sought an ally, Miss Hisaye Yamamoto, Nisei Correspondent for the *Los Angeles Tribune*. She is a remarkable and resilient woman, a survivor like myself of the so-called American justice system. Unfortunately, her best efforts have compromised our direct action with personal complications. I may have to stay in Los Angeles longer than expected.

HISAYE: There's nothing personal about it.

BAYARD: You had a drink with him, Miss Able Grable.

HISAYE: At your urging! You winked at me!

BAYARD: If everyone did my bidding when I winked at them, everything would be copasetic. Should I wink at Señor Remedios?

HISAYE: I care not. He thinks love is science! Math!

BAYARD: Love is patient and kind.

HISAYE: Don't quote First Corinthians to me!

BAYARD: Love doesn't envy or boast, isn't arrogant or rude. Love doesn't insist on its own way—

HISAYE: Love doesn't sit on its ass!

*(Shocked silence for a moment, then both* BAYARD *and* HISAYE *laugh.)*

BAYARD: We've both struck out. We need a pinch hitter.

HISAYE: No one else from the paper—

BAYARD: Someone from the ofay segment of the population.

HISAYE: Don't quote me to me. It puts me in a bad humor.

BAYARD: On the Journey of Reconciliation and at other sit-ins and direct actions, we do best side-by-side with sympathetic Caucasians. Have you heard of Everett C. Maxwell?

HISAYE: Who's that?

BAYARD: An art critic and screenwriter.

HISAYE: *(Shakes head)* We need someone of unimpeachable character.

BAYARD: We need a white person.

HISAYE: I resent looking to white people to be our heroes.

BAYARD: But sometimes they come in handy.

HISAYE: And he's agreed to help us?

BAYARD: Absolutely!

*(Lights up on* EVERETT.*)*

EVERETT: Absolutely not!

BAYARD: I merely need to advise him of the details.

*(Lights out on* BAYARD *and* HISAYE.*)*

EVERETT: Interior: bar. Clifton's Pacific Seas Tiki Bar is a Polynesian nightmare. Maxwell quietly nurses a Mai Tai. The paper umbrella reminds him of *ukiyo-e* prints from the Edo Period. He contemplates Japanese art and the bargains available these days, with servicemen returning to California from Tokyo. War booty. *(Twirls the umbrella)* War booty. *(He's obviously had more than one cocktail.)* Maxwell remembers purchasing Edo Period prints for the Museum. Before the First World War. Before everything degenerated. Before…

*(Lights up on* ZENOBIO.*)*

ZENOBIO: Staff is prepared for Miss Yamamoto to return to Bimini Baths. I anticipate reinforcements since she was not able to infiltrate by herself.

*(Lights up on* HISAYE.*)*

HISAYE: Mr Rustin's brainchild was doomed. Our Caucasian collaborator was not the type of gentleman given to direct action. A fuddy duddy of wealth and privilege, as Rustin described him. I am becoming impatient with passive resistance. You have to do something or nothing changes! Get off your ass and jump! Otherwise what are we here for?

*(*BAYARD *joins* EVERETT *in the bar.)*

BAYARD: How many of those manly little tropicocktails have you had?

EVERETT: Just this one! *(Out)* Maxwell gestures. Rustin sits.

BAYARD: You look like you've been island hopping.

EVERETT: Ask the bartender!

BAYARD: You've certainly been bar hopping. I've traced your Journey of Inebriation through four increasingly down-low establishments.

EVERETT: I've no idea what you're talking about.

BAYARD: I need your help tomorrow.

EVERETT: Tomorrow?!

BAYARD: So sober up.

EVERETT: I told you I can't.

BAYARD: They post the same gimpy vet at the door every day. Zenobio Remedios is certainly too young to remember whatever it is you did at Bimini in 1916.

EVERETT: Zenobio Remedios?

BAYARD: If you get to know him well enough, I hear he lets you call him Zeno. A good little soldier who needs very badly to get fucked.

EVERETT: *Ay, dios mio!*

BAYARD: I assume he speaks Spanish.

EVERETT: Maxwell is stunned.

BAYARD: But he didn't start working there until almost twenty years after your last visit.

EVERETT: Rustin stands.

BAYARD: Why are you narrating?

EVERETT: *(Out)* Maxwell is startled. *(To* BAYARD*)* What?

BAYARD: Man, you're soused. You're talking to people who aren't there.

EVERETT: *(Gestures toward audience)* Take a gander.

*(*BAYARD *looks into the audience, doesn't seem to see them.)*

BAYARD: Jeepers.

EVERETT: They come to observe. To be entertained. To escape.

BAYARD: No more Mai Tais for you.

EVERETT: They see you. They hear you. They know you. Your desperate need to be…tolerated.

BAYARD: I don't want to be tolerated! I want to be loved!

EVERETT: *(To audience)* Could you love him?

*(*EVERETT, *very drunk, takes careful steps toward the audience as* BAYARD *watches with alarm.)*

ZENOBIO: It is my professional duty to report that this may not be an appropriate assignment—for me. I have violated policy by meeting with one of the agitators privately, and my actions may have compromised—

BAYARD: Everett, what are you doing?

ZENOBIO: *I may be compromised.*

HISAYE: This is my column, I can say what I want, but I promised never to lie to you, dear reader, so—

ZENOBIO: Personally compromised.

EVERETT: *(To an audience member)* He's a persuasive Negro, isn't he?

HISAYE: —I confess that I may be jeopardizing my journalistic integrity—

BAYARD: *(Going to* EVERETT *in the audience)* Don't—that isn't going to help—

HISAYE: I think I may have let myself become the story.

ZENOBIO: But I am prepared.

EVERETT: He commands attention, don't you think!

BAYARD: *(To audience member)* I'm sorry—he's been drinking—

HISAYE: They say put your heart in your work, but I've bungled it. Could I go extravagantly mad like Miss Sakiyama? Sexually insane?

ZENOBIO: When they come, we have a plan.

EVERETT: He wants me to do something simple.

BAYARD: *(Trying to pull* EVERETT *away)* Goodness, this is awkward.

HISAYE:*(Going into the audience)* Dear reader, I'm torn. This is a story everybody needs to know, but—

ZENOBIO: Management has a plan. It's very simple.

*(Their dialogue overlaps, runs together, as everyone but* ZENOBIO *infiltrates the audience.)*

EVERETT: Very simple. Just bathe myself. Be baptized! Cleansed!

BAYARD: Tell him he can do it. Maybe he'll listen to you.

HISAYE: —I don't want to betray his trust. Nor yours. You trust me, don't you?

ZENOBIO: It's all perfectly legal.

EVERETT: He doesn't know the truth. I can't tell him. But let me tell you. It's terrible.

BAYARD: He just needs to go with us to the Baths. Stand with us.

HISAYE: You trust me to tell the whole story, even the unlovely parts. The parts I didn't know—

*(All except* ZENOBIO *may reach out to audience members, touch them. It's uncomfortable and freaky.)*

ZENOBIO: It's my job.

EVERETT: Terrible. The worst thing!

BAYARD: I've been arrested dozens of times. It couldn't be worse than that. What could be worse than prison?

EVERETT: Worse! Beyond redemption!

BAYARD: Tell him.

HISAYE: I didn't know. How could I know?

ZENOBIO: My duty.

EVERETT: I could die of it. Drown in the cleansing waters!

BAYARD: Please tell him. He has to help.

HISAYE: And I've fallen in love with him! With my story! His broken foot broke my heart.

BAYARD: Tell him why what we do tomorrow will change the world forever! Tell him!

EVERETT: He can't baptize me.

ZENOBIO: Duty. That's more important than she is, isn't it?

HISAYE: How inexplicably stupid! Love!

BAYARD: Who are you talking about, Everett?

ZENOBIO: Just follow orders.

EVERETT: I can't see him!

HISAYE: He trusts me. He said call him—

BAYARD: Can't see who?

EVERETT & HISAYE: Zeno!

BAYARD: Zeno?

ZENOBIO: I'm figuring out the science, doing the math. Hate. That's the cause of all the trouble in the world: cruel words, lynchings, wars. How many individuals do you personally hate? Count 'em. Not many, is it? Now how many do you love? Your parents, your sister, your brother, your wife, your husband, children, boyfriend, girlfriend. All those people you love— *(Weighs with hands)* —And maybe a handful you hate. Love should outweigh hate, outnumber it. Science. Math. Love. A simple calculation.

*(Sees the others staring at him)*

ZENOBIO: Isn't it?

## END OF ACT ONE

# ACT TWO

*(Four lights isolate the following objects on stage: a guitar,* HISAYE's *notebook, the baculum, and a strip of cloth.* HISAYE *approaches an audience member.)*

HISAYE: *(Confidentially)* Let me tell you a story.

*(*EVERETT *approaches an audience member. He is no longer drunk.)*

EVERETT: May I read you my screenplay?

*(*BAYARD *approaches an audience member.)*

BAYARD: I can tell you this with a clear conscience.

*(*ZENOBIO *approaches an audience member.)*

ZENOBIO: You're keen to be in the know, aren't you?

*(Their confiding conversations with audience members segue slowly back onto the stage.)*

HISAYE: Are you familiar with the Indian epic, *The Mahabharata*? It's the Hindu history of India: the gods, goddesses, and mortals. There's a narrative thread, a grand theme, but along the way, many stories. Passed down over generations through oral tradition, the epic grow'd like Topsy, with new stories, new points of view nestling themselves inside until it was more than just the history of India. *(Reaches the stage, picks up the notebook)* It was the story of everything.

BAYARD: I've been arrested, thrown in jail, spent months in prison, endured crude insults and animal names, been threatened, beat up, interrogated, and publicly humiliated. I fought for civil rights all my life, fought for justice, fought for peace. *Fought* for peace! But I never worked so hard in manifold ways against so many obstacles as I did for our direct action at Bimini Baths. *(Reaches stage, picks up guitar)* And one of those obstacles was me. *(He strums guitar under.)*

EVERETT: Interior: Vestibule. Rustin strums a guitar. A young Japanese woman makes notes in an elegant, leather-bound notebook. It's early morning. The entrance to Bimini Baths is quiet. *(Reaches stage, picks up cloth, worries it)* For now. Cut to:

ZENOBIO: February 19, 1948. Bimini Baths daily admissions log.

EVERETT: Close up: Zenobio Remedios. Forty-four years of age, war-weary, jaw tightened for his onerous task.

ZENOBIO: As expected, protestors Mr Rustin and Miss Yamamoto appeared and requested entry to the facility.

| | |
|---|---|
| HISAYE: I would like admission to the plunge, a scalp massage and facial treatment, please— | BAYARD: May I have the course of twenty-one Bimini Treatments with time limit—? |

*(ZENOBIO reaches the stage, picks up the bone, slapping it nervously again his palm.)*

BAYARD & HISAYE: Mr Remedios?

EVERETT: Medium shot. Remedios slaps an object against his palm. What is it?

ZENOBIO: May I see your health certificates? *(Slips bone in his pocket)*

BAYARD: Our what certificates?

ZENOBIO: Health certificates.

HISAYE: Is that a new requirement?

ZENOBIO: In an effort to prevent the spread of poliomyelitis and to protect its patrons, Bimini Baths and Natural Hot Spring Resort has instituted an admissions policy requiring certificates issued by the County Health Department.

HISAYE: That's completely arbitrary!

ZENOBIO: Not arbitrary—*sanitary*.

BAYARD: This is the same old business. Your policy didn't exist until we requested admittance.

ZENOBIO: We must be strict about our policy. It protects everyone from polio. You wouldn't want to end up in an iron lung.

HISAYE: Zeno!

BAYARD: Si, let Mr Remedios make a chucklehead of himself trying to justify his absurd and instantly fabricated policy—

ZENOBIO: It's not mine!

HISAYE: Of course it isn't—!

BAYARD: Do you stand behind it or not?

EVERETT: Remedios is silent for a moment.

ZENOBIO: *(After a moment)* Do you have your certificates?

HISAYE: Of course not, don't be silly.

BAYARD: Would we need certificates if we came back on Mexican Day?

EVERETT: Remedios is silent.

HISAYE: The health of Mexicans is not a concern?

ZENOBIO: I'm not authorized to debate our policy with you, Miss Yamamoto.

HISAYE: Very well.

BAYARD & HISAYE: *(Out)* We had no choice.

EVERETT: They sit. Maxwell observes from a distance, unseen by Remedios.

(BAYARD *and* HISAYE *situate themselves elegantly upon the floor.*)

ZENOBIO: The police have been summoned.

BAYARD: And the press? Will you also summon the press so you can explain to a crush of reporters your racial policy?

HISAYE: The press—

EVERETT: Yamamoto pulls out her notebook.

HISAYE: —Is already here.

EVERETT: Wait…that notebook…

BAYARD: Would you like an interview?

HISAYE: Eventually. But we have plenty of time.

EVERETT: How'd she get that notebook?

ZENOBIO: Officers will be here pronto.

EVERETT: It was sealed!

ZENOBIO: Hang it up. You're obstructing our business and for that you can go to jail.

EVERETT: I can't—stay—!

HISAYE: What's jail like, Mr Rustin?

EVERETT: *(Out)* Maxwell—leaves! *(He does.)*

BAYARD: As many times as I've been the guest of government hospitality, I can say with some authority I do not recommend it.

HISAYE: *(Making notes)* And why is that?

BAYARD: I'm afraid our country's local jails and even state penitentiaries are a law unto themselves. A man like me or sadly, even a woman like you, is unprotected, at the mercy of often merciless men. I once saw a Negro woman hanged in her cell. They claimed she did it herself.

HISAYE: I'm familiar with government hospitality—

BAYARD: That's right! The American Dachau!

ZENOBIO: Dachau!

HISAYE: *(Nervous)* Not Dachau exactly, but—

ZENOBIO: What'd you tell him?

HISAYE: No details—just—

BAYARD: You liberated Dachau. You're a hero.

ZENOBIO: That was personal!

HISAYE: Did you have to say—?

ZENOBIO: I told you in confidence!

BAYARD: Mr Remedios, she is the press. Nothing's in confidence. Everything is written down. *(After a moment)* Don't go into a decline.

HISAYE: You're flirting with him at my expense. Not everyone's an invert.

BAYARD: They are after I get through with them.

HISAYE: Shhhh!

BAYARD: *(Looks around, to* HISAYE*)* Where's Everett?

HISAYE: *(To* BAYARD*)* We can't do much till he comes.

ZENOBIO: It's rude to whisper.

BAYARD: We'd be more than happy to engage you in conversation, Mr Remedios—

HISAYE: Flirting!

BAYARD: Miss Yamamoto is writing all of this down.

HISAYE: Not all of it…

BAYARD: I've been doing a little writing myself. *(Strums guitar)* Do you enjoy Renaissance music?

ZENOBIO: *Ay, dios mio.*

HISAYE: I'm more of a Romantic girl.

BAYARD: Perhaps you already know *The Ballad of Bimini Baths.*

HISAYE: Yes, but it never loses its charm.

ZENOBIO: You eager beavers ever give up?

BAYARD & HISAYE: Nope!

BAYARD: *(Strums guitar and sings)*
At Bimini the springs are hot
A pure and natural flow
The mineral waters purge and clean
The guests as white as snow

ZENOBIO: Roll up your flaps! You'll provoke the patrons.

BAYARD: *(Sings)*
Not everyone is welcome there
So check before you go
Are you the kind who mingles with

BAYARD & HISAYE: *(Singing)*
The guests as white as snow?

*(EVERETT appears with a change of costume playing CARLYLE. EVERETT AS CARLYLE glances at HISAYE and BAYARD then proceeds to ZENOBIO.)*

EVERETT AS CARLYLE: *(New York accent)* Morning, Xavier.

ZENOBIO: Good morning, Mr Carlyle.

EVERETT AS CARLYLE: Why you working the door, Xavier? Anything to do with—? *(Jerks his head toward BAYARD and HISAYE)*

HISAYE: His name is Zenobio.

ZENOBIO: *(Quickly, overlapping)* The usual treatments, sir?

EVERETT AS CARLYLE: Not so good for the reputation, Hooverville at your door.

ZENOBIO: The police are on the way. We have a new Hamamelis Rub, if you'd be interested—

EVERETT AS CARLYLE: Not Hooverville—*Bronze*ville!

ZENOBIO: Your usual treatments plus general admission is seventy-five cents.

EVERETT AS CARLYLE: *(Giving* ZENOBIO *the money)* Hope you put the kibosh on that by the time I'm done. Not something you wanna see more than once, if you know what I mean.

ZENOBIO: I do, Mr Carlyle.

EVERETT AS CARLYLE: Good boy, Xavier.

BAYARD & HISAYE: Zenobio!

*(*EVERETT AS CARLYLE *disappears inside Bimini Baths.)*

ZENOBIO: You're gonna cost us business!

BAYARD: Good people will indeed turn away when made aware of your policies.

HISAYE: How many times has he been here and he can't remember your name?

ZENOBIO: What he's gonna remember is the snafu in the vestibule!

BAYARD: *(Sings)*
Señor Remedios was brave
And valiant in the war
But found his biggest battle yet
The guardpost at the door

ZENOBIO: Quit beating your gums!

HISAYE: He'll stop if you let us in.

ZENOBIO: You're making it sound like it's me!

HISAYE: Exactly, Zeno—it's not you—

(EVERETT *appears as* TRUDY, *a fashionable matron with a Southern accent.*)

EVERETT AS TRUDY: Oh!

ZENOBIO: Good afternoon, Mrs. Henderson.

(BAYARD *and* HISAYE *stare her down, but after a moment she goes to* ZENOBIO.)

EVERETT AS TRUDY: Zeno, have I made a terrible mistake?

ZENOBIO: No, ma'am. What do you mean?

EVERETT AS TRUDY: It's not Mexican Day, is it?

ZENOBIO: No, ma'am, it's a regular day.

EVERETT AS TRUDY: I come here to relax, to feel clean.

ZENOBIO: We won't permit them to enter.

EVERETT AS TRUDY: I should hope not. That wouldn't be safe. Could I have the electric cabinet bath plus shampoo and scalp massage?

ZENOBIO: Of course. That'll be three dollars and twenty-five cents.

EVERETT AS TRUDY: (*Giving him the money*) They can't really afford to enter anyway, can they? Poverty is a problem in our country, but in this case— (*Quick glance at* HISAYE *and* BAYARD) —It's a mercy!

(EVERETT AS TRUDY *disappears into the Baths.*)

ZENOBIO: You see? You're not gaining any sympathizers.

HISAYE: And yet we're still here.

ZENOBIO: It's almost closing. Aren't you running out of gas?

BAYARD: (*Sings*)
The first day dragged from dawn to dusk
But none will budge so far

A protest song played pleasantly
Upon a small guitar

(EVERETT *appears as* OFFICER OLSON. *He studies* BAYARD
*and* HISAYE *for a moment, then proceeds to* ZENOBIO.)

EVERETT AS OFFICER OLSON: *(Scandinavian accent)* Did
you call in the complaint?

ZENOBIO: Yes, sir.

EVERETT AS OFFICER OLSON: Any damage to the
property?

ZENOBIO: No, but obstruction as you see—

EVERETT AS OFFICER OLSON: They giving your
customers flak or inconveniencing them in any way?

ZENOBIO: Several patrons have made mention.

EVERETT AS OFFICER OLSON: I can't arrest them on a
mention.

ZENOBIO: They're scaring people away. Hurting our
trade!

(EVERETT AS OFFICER OLSON *turns to look at* BAYARD *and*
HISAYE. *They smile sweetly.*)

EVERETT AS OFFICER OLSON: They don't look so
intimidating.

ZENOBIO: But—!

(BAYARD *gives a quick strum to the guitar.*)

EVERETT AS OFFICER OLSON: And you get free live
music.

ZENOBIO: I could lose my job!

EVERETT AS OFFICER OLSON: Don't call unless there's a
real beef.

(EVERETT AS OFFICER OLSON *saunters out. As* BAYARD
*sings, the lights go out on* HISAYE *and* ZENOBIO.)

BAYARD: *(Sings)*
At Bimini the springs are pure
Protected by Jim Crow
But what can wash your conscience clean
With guests as white as snow?
*(Speaking)* February 20, 1948. On the fourth day of our direct action, the admission desk was manned by Mr J J Warrick, the owner of Bimini Baths.

*(Lighting change reveals* EVERETT AS WARRICK *where* ZENOBIO *had been previously.)*

BAYARD: Do you not trust Mr Remedios to keep us out?

EVERETT AS WARRICK: White people won't come if we let you in. Simple as that. My own personal feelings don't enter into it. Come back on Mexican Day and you're welcome to it! Only twenty-five cents!

*(*HISAYE *appears as* YASUNARI, *dressed in the quasi-medical uniform of Bimini Baths [different from* ZENOBIO's*].)*

EVERETT AS WARRICK: Yasunari, what're you doing here?

HISAYE AS YASUNARI: Good morning Mr Warrick. I came to see— *(Gestures to* BAYARD*)*

EVERETT AS WARRICK: You never seen a Negro before?

HISAYE AS YASUNARI: Not here in our vestibule. *(To* BAYARD*)* You're ruining our business. Please go home.

EVERETT AS WARRICK: Now, Yasunari, cool down.

HISAYE AS YASUNARI: I said please.

EVERETT AS WARRICK: He'll get bored soon enough.

HISAYE AS YASUNARI: You're making trouble for all of us. There are plenty of places around town for you.

EVERETT AS WARRICK: Or come back next Thursday! Two Roosevelts and a Jefferson!

HISAYE AS YASUNARI: Listen to the boss man! The colored staff doesn't want you here!

BAYARD: I understand. You need the work. You can't protest your own job.

HISAYE AS YASUNARI: I don't want to protest!

BAYARD: I'm doing it for you.

HISAYE AS YASUNARI: Kurombo!

EVERETT AS WARRICK: It's hunky dory, Yasunari. Come inside and get to work.

HISAYE AS YASUNARI: Sorry, Mr Warrick. *(Starts to enter)*

EVERETT AS WARRICK: Staff entrance.

HISAYE AS YASUNARI: Sorry, sir, staff entrance.

*(HISAYE AS YASUNARI leaves the way he came in. ZENOBIO enters as SANTOS, also dressed in the Bimini staff uniform. He sees BAYARD.)*

ZENOBIO AS SANTOS: *Ay, chingado.* [Ay, fucker]

BAYARD: *Buenos dias.* [Good day]

EVERETT AS WARRICK: Ignore him, Santos.

ZENOBIO AS SANTOS: Who are you?

BAYARD: *(Standing, shaking hands)* Bayard Rustin. Your name is Santos?

ZENOBIO AS SANTOS: Francisco Maximilian Castro de Santos.

BAYARD: *Mucho gusto.* [Nice to meet you]

EVERETT AS WARRICK: Santos!

ZENOBIO: Should I remove him, Mr Warrick? Rough him up?

BAYARD: I wouldn't mind that.

EVERETT AS WARRICK: No!

BAYARD: Are you related to Zenobio Remedios?

ZENOBIO AS SANTOS: We all look alike.

BAYARD: Exactly alike. *Muy guapo.* [Very handsome]

ZENOBIO AS SANTOS: *Y tu.* [You, too]

BAYARD: *Tu entiendes.* [You understand]

ZENOBIO AS SANTOS: *Si, entiendo.* [Yes, I understand]

EVERETT AS WARRICK: Santos!

*(With a smile at* BAYARD, ZENOBIO AS SANTOS *disappears.)*

EVERETT AS WARRICK: Don't talk to my staff or I'll have you arrested for indecency.

BAYARD: *Habla Espanol?*

EVERETT AS WARRICK: No, but I'm not blind. Goddamn Communist.

*(*HISAYE *appears as herself.)*

HISAYE: Good afternoon, Bayard. Ready for a shift change?

BAYARD: Si, darling!

HISAYE: Dearest!

*(*BAYARD *plants one on her.* EVERETT AS WARRICK *looks confused.)*

EVERETT AS WARRICK: Hey!

HISAYE: *(Quietly)* What was that about?

BAYARD: I'm fucking with Mr Warrick, here.

HISAYE: And with me! I feel like everything's getting all mixed up. I don't know who's who any more.

BAYARD: Exciting, isn't it? *(Hands her the guitar)* Keep confusing him.

HISAYE: Enjoy your evening.

BAYARD: Good night. *(He leaves.)*

EVERETT AS WARRICK: That your boyfriend?

(ZENOBIO *arrives.*)

HISAYE: Everyone's always asking me that! No!

ZENOBIO: Hello.

HISAYE: Hello.

EVERETT AS WARRICK: Zeno, take over the door.

ZENOBIO: Of course, Mr Warrick.

EVERETT AS WARRICK: I know this is hard on you, Zeno, and I appreciate you going the extra mile.

ZENOBIO: Thank you, sir.

EVERETT AS WARRICK: They don't make it easy.

(EVERETT AS WARRICK *leaves.* HISAYE *and* ZENOBIO *look at each other then don't. After a bit,* HISAYE *strums the guitar, not as expert as* BAYARD. BAYARD *appears as* NATRICK, *also in the Bimini uniform.)*

BAYARD AS NATRICK: *(Jamaican accent)* Coo yah!

ZENOBIO: Leave her alone, Natrick.

BAYARD AS NATRICK: Ease up on yourself. I'm not doing nothing.

ZENOBIO: Your shift is starting.

BAYARD AS NATRICK: But this here lady blocking my way.

HISAYE: I don't mean to block you, Mr Natrick. But I am happy my presence does not go unnoticed.

BAYARD AS NATRICK: What are you trying to do?

HISAYE: Have a dip in the plunge and a treatment or two. *(Refers to brochure)* What's a Nauheim bath?

BAYARD AS NATRICK: That's the Hydrotherapy Department. I'm in Electro Therapy.

HISAYE: May I interview you for the *Los Angeles Tribune*? It's a Negro paper.

ZENOBIO: No!

HISAYE: Mr Remedios, I'm sure Mr Natrick can make up his own mind about speaking to the press.

BAYARD AS NATRICK: She ready.

ZENOBIO: Warrick would fire you, Natrick, so fast.

BAYARD AS NATRICK: *(After a moment)* She eat under sheet?

HISAYE: What?

ZENOBIO: Natrick, one more word and you're reported.

(BAYARD AS NATRICK *signs something nasty and leaves.*)

HISAYE: He was willing!

ZENOBIO: He has a reputation for disrespect. Charming and professional to the white ladies, but…

HISAYE: I see. Thank you.

(EVERETT *appears.*)

HISAYE: There you are!

EVERETT: Where'd you get that notebook, if I may ask?

HISAYE: My uncle found it in the trash where he works.

EVERETT: Where's that?

HISAYE: The County Courthouse.

EVERETT: It looks old.

HISAYE: I'm sure it's not a rare book or anything valuable like that.  The first owner used it as a diary, so I tore those pages out.

EVERETT: Did you read them?

HISAYE: After the first few lines I realized it was very private so I put it in a box and forgot about it. I'm not a journalist all the time!

ZENOBIO: May I help you, sir?

EVERETT: Um…

HISAYE: Go ahead!

EVERETT: *(Goes to* ZENOBIO*)* I'd like to purchase admission to the plunge for one.

ZENOBIO: Certainly, sir. If you'll give me your name we can set up an account to keep track of your treatments and payments.

EVERETT: Just one visit.

ZENOBIO: We have to be very strict these days for the health and safety of our patrons. Name?

EVERETT: *(After a moment)* Maxwell.

ZENOBIO: *(Writing)* First name, Mr Maxwell?

EVERETT: Everett.

*(*ZENOBIO *stops writing and looks at* EVERETT *as if seeing him clearly for the first time.)*

ZENOBIO: Mr Maxwell.

EVERETT: That's correct. May I enter?

ZENOBIO: Everett Maxwell.

EVERETT: Yes.

ZENOBIO: Who's the best artist in the world?

EVERETT: I beg your pardon?

*(*ZENOBIO *puts his wrists together above his head as if bound.)*

ZENOBIO: Who am I?

EVERETT: I'm sorry—I'm sorry— *(Stumbles away from* ZENOBIO*)* I can't—

ZENOBIO: You know! I'm a martyr!

EVERETT: *(Passes by* HISAYE*)* Miss, tell Bayard I can't—I have to—

HISAYE: Everett, what's wrong?

ZENOBIO: A saint—!

HISAYE: I'm so confused. You know Zeno?

EVERETT: No—no—I thought I could, but—I can't—

ZENOBIO: You're all in cahoots!

(EVERETT *runs out.*)

HISAYE: *(After a moment)* Now you won't even let white people in?

ZENOBIO: I didn't turn him away. He ran off.

HISAYE: And you know him?

ZENOBIO: I can't tell you anything. You write it all down.

HISAYE: My shift ends at ten. Yours?

ZENOBIO: You know Mr Maxwell?

HISAYE: Bayard does.

ZENOBIO: Does he have his telephone number?

HISAYE: Come get a drink after work.

ZENOBIO: No, I have to find Mr Maxwell. Your friend is—?

HISAYE: Bayard Rustin. And you want his number.

*(Lights out on* ZENOBIO.*)*

HISAYE: When I was in high school, one of our farm workers contrived to follow me to the outhouse. I'm sure I gave him some secret message, a hesitation, a glance back, that told him I might welcome his pursuit. And I did welcome it for a moment, let him into the dank darkness of the biffy, but his soft lips and rough cheek and hard fingers shocked me so much I stumbled quickly away, back to the house before my parents even noticed I was gone. I never let him in again. That encounter, that collision in the privy, affected me beyond the frantic fumbling in the dark, left me with an—awkwardness—around men, an aggressive ambivalence that's always confused them, and me. I'm finally ready once again to let someone in, and he turns me down to pursue a homosexual who keeps kissing me, an even larger perplexity. You think you've figured someone out, then they do something that doesn't fit.

*(Lights out on* HISAYE *and up on* ZENOBIO.*)*

ZENOBIO: February 21, 1948. At the beginning of my shift Mr Warrick gave me a pep talk.

*(*BAYARD *appears as* WARRICK, *with the same costume piece and mannerisms as when* EVERETT *played* WARRICK.*)*

BAYARAD AS WARRICK: Zeno, I'm proud of you. Seeing you at the admissions desk, an American soldier doing his job, his duty, it inspires me. Cause that's what we do here in America, our jobs. Nothing's more important than that, meeting our obligations, doing what we say we'll do. And when you took this job—

ZENOBIO: I'm only in admissions on a temporary basis, Mr Warrick.

BAYARAD AS WARRICK: But you take your responsibilities seriously, accept them, no second guessing, no false loyalties, just doing your job.

ZENOBIO: False loyalties?

BAYARAD AS WARRICK: Well, for instance, one might think—I never would, but some—some might think those protesters would see you as one of them. But you're one of us, and that's why I put you at the door.

ZENOBIO: I do my job, sir. I've always been like that.

BAYARAD AS WARRICK: American through and through. I was sad to see you shipped off to Europe but proud as if you were my own son.

ZENOBIO: Thank you, Mr Warrick.

BAYARAD AS WARRICK: If we beat the whole Imperial Fleet in the Pacific, we can handle one little geisha in our foyer.

ZENOBIO: She's American as me.

BAYARAD AS WARRICK: Zeno, don't say that! You may be Mexican on the outside, but inside you're the 42nd Rainbow Division of the United States Army!

ZENOBIO: Thank you, sir.

BAYARAD AS WARRICK: You're on the right side of this. Come back next Thursday and have a dip on me: *(Hands* ZENOBIO *some coins)* Two Roosevelts and a Jefferson!

*(Lighting shift.* BAYARD *turns back into himself, putting both* BAYARD *and* ZENOBIO *in a night club, drinks in hand.* ZENOBIO *is keyed up,* BAYARD *energized and excited.)*

ZENOBIO: I'm not on your side.

BAYARD: What side is that?

ZENOBIO: The—you know—the colored side.

BAYARD: The Mexican side? The side that can use the plunge this coming Thursday? I'm looking forward to it, but I guess you can't join us in the frolic.

ZENOBIO: You're kind of an asshole.

BAYARD: You're kind of drunk.

ZENOBIO: Not as drunk as you'd like.

BAYARD: I'm a patient man.

ZENOBIO: How do you know Everett Maxwell?

BAYARD: I met him at the museum.

ZENOBIO: Me, too.

BAYARD: He used to work there.

ZENOBIO: Do you have his telephone number?

BAYARD: Wouldn't give it to me. Very hush-hush. Said he might visit me at my hotel.

ZENOBIO: I wanna show him something.

BAYARD: And I thought you wanted to have a drink with me. I'm as confused as Si.

ZENOBIO: She snapped her cap cause I asked for your number.

BAYARD: You dragged me to the Cobra Club just to brown her off?

ZENOBIO: You remind me of a cat I used to work with.

BAYARD: At the Baths?

ZENOBIO: Yeah.

BAYARD: Negro?

ZENOBIO: Yeah. A real joker.

BAYARD: Where's he now?

ZENOBIO: The war.

BAYARD: You miss him?

(ZENOBIO *shrugs.*)

BAYARD: You miss him.

(BAYARD *touches* ZENOBIO, *who doesn't react at all. Lights out on them and up on* EVERETT.)

EVERETT: Cut to: Exterior. Dunbar Hotel on Central Avenue. Laughter and jazz spill out onto the street. Maxwell stands in a pool of blinking neon, his skin a canvas alternately green then blue then green.

*(Lights up on* HISAYE.)

HISAYE: Almena Davis, Editor-in-Chief (and I do mean In Chief) of the *Los Angeles Tribune*, gives me free rein in this column most of the time. But:

(ZENOBIO *appears as* ALMENA DAVIS.)

ZENOBIO AS ALMENA: Miss Yamamoto.

HISAYE: Miss Davis.

ZENOBIO AS ALMENA: I understand Bayard Rustin was here the other day.

HISAYE: I had the privilege of making his acquaintance.

ZENOBIO AS ALMENA: Did he say what he's in town for?

HISAYE: To ask our help with a nonviolent direct action at Bimini Baths.

ZENOBIO AS ALMENA: I see. Are we helping?

HISAYE: I haven't been of much help yet, but I'm hopeful we'll prevail.

ZENOBIO AS ALMENA: That's not our role. We are journalists.

HISAYE: I want to write about it in *Small Talk*.

ZENOBIO AS ALMENA: I always give you complete freedom—

HISAYE: I know, and I'm most grateful—

ZENOBIO AS ALMENA: You're becoming the story. I won't be accused of creating news.

HISAYE: I can't stand by like we did when Mr Short asked for our help.

ZENOBIO AS ALMENA: You made that decision.

HISAYE: Based on the Tribune's guidelines!

ZENOBIO AS ALMENA: Objectivity gives journalism its authority!

HISAYE: Journalistic objectivity supports authority, reinforces the status quo. Objectivity let a Negro family burn to death in Fontana!

ZENOBIO AS ALMENA: Miss Yamamoto, I know you enjoy writing your column—

HISAYE: *(Gritted teeth)* Yes, I enjoy it!

ZENOBIO AS ALMENA: And I want you to enjoy it for years to come, but you're willfully disobeying our policy—

HISAYE: Disobeying?!

ZENOBIO AS ALMENA: I'm sorry, that sounds harsh, but—

HISAYE: I quit!

ZENOBIO AS ALMENA: What?

HISAYE: *(Gathering her things)* My own journalistic integrity is to tell the truth, even if the truth is me. I love writing for the Tribune, but you're saying I can't take action, I can only document. I do not wish to observe the pain of innocent people while doing nothing.

ZENOBIO AS ALMENA: Writing is not nothing!

HISAYE: It's worse than nothing if the words don't turn into deeds. It's immoral to document a death when you could save a life.

ZENOBIO AS ALMENA: Where are you going?

HISAYE: To Bimini Baths! I'd invite you to join me, but I guess you won't come until Mexican Day!

*(Lights out on* HISAYE *and* ZENOBIO AS ALMENA.*)*

EVERETT: Close-up: Maxwell's blue/green face as he decides to go into the hotel. Will Rustin let him in?

*(*BAYARD *appears in a robe.* BAYARD *and* EVERETT *are in his hotel room.)*

BAYARD: The Pageant of the Masters?

EVERETT: I believe you'd enjoy it very much. *Tableaux vivantes* at the beach.

BAYARD: *Tableaux* of what?

EVERETT: *(Strikes a crucifixion pose)* Great works of art.

BAYARD: Which beach?

EVERETT: Laguna.

BAYARD: They let Negroes go down there?

EVERETT: Has that ever stopped you?

BAYARD: Si said you ran away. Why?

EVERETT: You wouldn't understand.

BAYARD: Would you like a drink?

EVERETT: Yes, actually!

BAYARD: Take a load off.

EVERETT: Maxwell sits, trembling. He needs that drink.

BAYARD: *(Fixing drinks)* This horrid secret—

EVERETT: Rustin pours drinks.

BAYARD: *(Hands* EVERETT *a drink)* —Have you ever told anyone?

EVERETT: Someone I shouldn't have trusted.

BAYARD: Who?

EVERETT: A psychiatrist.

BAYARD: Me, too.

EVERETT: You went to a head-shrinker?

BAYARD: He came to me. In prison.

EVERETT: Me, too.

BAYARD: To psychiatrists. And prison.

*(*BAYARD *and* EVERETT *toast and drink. Lights out on them and up on* HISAYE.*)*

HISAYE: Just as my confusion was becoming intolerable—

(ZENOBIO *appears.*)

HISAYE: He came to my apartment.

ZENOBIO: It's too late, isn't it?

HISAYE: And I let him in. (*She fixes drinks.*)

ZENOBIO: I figured it out. E = M L squared.

HISAYE: M L squared?

ZENOBIO: Energy equals the mass of people times the love you feel for them squared. By that formula, there should be more love in the world than hate.

HISAYE: That's a facile metaphor.

ZENOBIO: It's not a metaphor, it's math. You love more people than you hate, don't you?

HISAYE: Bayard was right. You're flirtatious after all.

ZENOBIO: I didn't mean—

HISAYE: Your theory doesn't hold up, Einstein. Some people hate folks they never met, thousands, millions. They hate Negroes, Mexicans, Japs, Jews.

ZENOBIO: I want to get clean! Don't you want to get clean?

HISAYE: Nobody in this dirty world has figured it out. But we have to try.

(*Lights up on* BAYARD *and* EVERETT.)

EVERETT: The music turns lush.

(*Languorous, sexy dance music plays.* EVERETT *strikes a pose.*)

BAYARD: Michelangelo's *David.*

(HISAYE *gives* ZENOBIO *a drink. She sits. He moves to another part of the room but remains standing awkwardly.*

*Lighting on* ZENOBIO *and* HISAYE *shifts.* BAYARD *strikes a pose.)*

EVERETT: *Discobolus.*

BAYARD: See? Who needs to go all the way to Laguna for *tableaux vivantes?*

*(*BAYARD *and* EVERETT *laugh and toast.)*

HISAYE: He stood awkwardly and quizzed me on old movies by a particular screenwriter.

ZENOBIO: *The Old Code?*

*(*HISAYE *shakes her head.* EVERETT *strikes a pose balancing on one foot.)*

BAYARD: I have no idea.

ZENOBIO: *Eyes of the Totem?*

*(*HISAYE *shakes her head.)*

EVERETT: I'm dancing.

BAYARD: Degas?

ZENOBIO: *The Heart of the Yukon?*

EVERETT & HISAYE: No!

HISAYE: I hate westerns.

EVERETT: Didn't you say you've been invited to India?

BAYARD: Oh, wait a minute—

ZENOBIO: He also writes about art, not just movies.

BAYARD: Krishna?

HISAYE: What kind of art?

EVERETT: Close!

BAYARD: Shiva?

ZENOBIO: All kinds.

EVERETT: Yes! Shiva—

BAYARD & EVERETT: —As Lord of the Dance!

ZENOBIO: There's even a picture of him in the County Museum.

EVERETT: One more, but I'll need your help.

(EVERETT *hands* BAYARD *the strip of cloth.*)

HISAYE: He sounds very accomplished.

BAYARD: Oh, no thanks.

HISAYE: Why is he afraid of you?

EVERETT: Not for you, for me.

ZENOBIO: He...taught me to swim at Bimini Baths.

BAYARD: I object to bondage on principle.

HISAYE: How old were you?

EVERETT: Just for the tableau. (*He crosses his wrists above his head.*)

ZENOBIO: Underage.

BAYARD: Just for the tableau.

(BAYARD *binds* EVERETT's *wrists.*)

HISAYE: Sixteen? Fifteen?

(ZENOBIO *gestures lower.*)

HISAYE: Fourteen?

ZENOBIO: Thirteen.

HISAYE: I see.

ZENOBIO: He was sent to San Quentin.

HISAYE: Oh, Zeno. Thirteen!

(HISAYE *goes to him and holds him.* BAYARD *steps back to observe* EVERETT, *who rolls his eyes heavenward.*)

BAYARD: Some martyr.

EVERETT: Redemption through suffering...

(HISAYE *and* ZENOBIO *start swaying to the music.*)

BAYARD: A saint.

EVERETT: Oscar Wilde's favorite.

BAYARD: Oh. St. Sebastian. Everyone knows that.

EVERETT: Not everyone.

(HISAYE *and* ZENOBIO *slow dance, sad and tender.* BAYARD *reaches for the cloth binding.*)

EVERETT: Leave it.

BAYARD: It makes me deeply uncomfortable.

EVERETT: Please.

(HISAYE *kisses* ZENOBIO. BAYARD *kisses* EVERETT.)

BAYARD: Does it hurt?

EVERETT: Close up: Maxwell's pale face. No one has touched him like this in thirty-two years.

BAYARD & HISAYE: You're crying.

EVERETT: Iris out.

(BAYARD *kisses* EVERETT *again as the light on them fades.* ZENOBIO *suddenly pushes away from* HISAYE.)

HISAYE: I'm sorry!

ZENOBIO: No, I'm sorry! I can't…dance. My foot.

HISAYE: Oh, I forgot. My apologies.

(HISAYE *and* ZENOBIO *stand there awkwardly.*)

ZENOBIO: It just…hurts a lot all of a sudden.

HISAYE: I understand. I think.

ZENOBIO: You're a very patient person. Kind.

HISAYE: Patient! I wish I could just jump!

ZENOBIO: I wish I could dance. It's not fair to you.

HISAYE: Zeno, I know you haven't written anything down—your story—

ZENOBIO: I can't—

HISAYE: But I would like to. Let me.

ZENOBIO: What?

HISAYE: Let me write it, Zeno. Let me in.

ZENOBIO: Let you in?

HISAYE: Let me in. Please.

ZENOBIO: No! I'm—sorry—! *(He rushes out.)*

HISAYE: And once again my aggressive ambivalence scotched my chance.

*(Lights out on* HISAYE *and up on* BAYARD.*)*

BAYARD: Dear Friend A J: The remarkable and persistent Miss Yamamoto has proven a complicated ally in our direct action, so I have enlisted another: the prominent art journalist and screenwriter, Everett Maxwell. He is highly intelligent and committed to our cause at great personal cost. He is also Caucasian, an advantage we will use as a flying wedge to gain admittance to the Baths.

*(*HISAYE *appears as* A J MUSTE.*)*

HISAYE AS A J: Dear Bayard: I was deeply distressed to learn that you've allied yourself with Mr Everett C Maxwell. I am trying to convince myself that you're unaware of his reprehensible criminal record. But I'm quite certain you know his moral failings and suspect that is one of the reasons you enrolled him. Bayard, Bayard, you are as a son to me, a great joy and a painful sorrow. Has the psychiatric counseling we paid for come to nothing? I urge you to step away from Bimini Baths before you damage not only your own already compromised reputation but also the civil rights movement as a whole. Let Los Angeles clean itself and do not dirty yourself on its behalf.

*(*HISAYE *becomes herself.)*

BAYARD & HISAYE: He's homosexual. *(A take)* I know.

HISAYE: Wait.

BAYARD: What?

BAYARD & HISAYE: Who are we talking about?

HISAYE: Zeno.

BAYARD: Everett.

HISAYE: Oh, I know that, too.

BAYARD: How do you know?

HISAYE: He told me.

BAYARD: Everett?

HISAYE: Zeno.

BAYARD: Zeno told you Everett's homosexual?

HISAYE: No. Yes. That, too.

BAYARD: I knew that. In fact—wait—what about Zeno?

HISAYE: He's homosexual.

BAYARD: Zeno said so?

HISAYE: Not in so many words.

BAYARD: But a woman knows.

HISAYE: When she kisses a man and he runs away, yes.

BAYARD: Everett didn't run away.

HISAYE: Don't brag. He's sixty years old.

BAYARD: Zeno told me he knew Everett from the Museum.

HISAYE: He knew him. Thirty-two years ago.

BAYARD: When Zeno was—

HISAYE: Thirteen.

BAYARD: He *knew* Everett? The same way I knew him last night?

HISAYE: I don't know. I wasn't there. Either time. But that's why he ran away.

BAYARD: Zeno.

HISAYE: Everett. He ran away when he saw Zeno at Bimini.

BAYARD: Everett went to prison thirty-two years ago. Because of Zeno?

HISAYE: *(Overlapping)* Because of Zeno.

BAYARD & HISAYE: Now it all makes sense.

*(Lights out on HISAYE and up on EVERETT.)*

BAYARD: How long were you in San Quentin?

EVERETT: A year.

BAYARD: I spent two years in Lewisburg Federal Penitentiary for draft resistance.

EVERETT: One year destroyed me.

BAYARD: I can't judge. That wasn't my only time in prison. And sex is my great weakness...

EVERETT: But.

BAYARD: A child.

EVERETT: Children.

BAYARD: More than one? Gracious!

EVERETT: So when I saw him at Bimini—

BAYARD: What did you do to them?

EVERETT: What you and I did.

BAYARD: *Tableaux vivantes?*

EVERETT: I raped them, Bayard!

BAYARD: It was statutory—

EVERETT: It was rape. I raped children. That's what I did. I will always be that monster who thirty years ago raped innocent boys. When you were threatened, imprisoned, beaten, you always knew you didn't deserve it. You always knew you were in the right. I know I was wrong.

BAYARD: Then come make it right.

EVERETT: Nothing can wash away that sin. My presence will only curse your efforts, doom them! *(Pause)* Rustin is silent. *(Pause)* I'm right. On this at least. You know I am.

*(Lights out on* EVERETT *and up on* HISAYE.*)*

BAYARD: If we…align ourselves only with the morally pure—

HISAYE: He's beyond impure—!

BAYARD: —We walk alone.

HISAYE: I'm with you.

BAYARD: Si, we've failed. Together, but we've failed.

HISAYE: Surely you let him off the hook, told him not to come.

BAYARD: So what do we do?

HISAYE: We sit.

BAYARD: On our asses.

HISAYE: Just a little longer than they can stand.

*(*BAYARD *and* HISAYE *sit. Lights up on* ZENOBIO *at the admissions desk of Bimini Baths.* ZENOBIO *ignores them, does paperwork.* BAYARD *quietly strums the guitar.* EVERETT *appears.* HISAYE *and* BAYARD *react but say nothing.* EVERETT *doesn't look at them.* ZENOBIO *sees him but goes quickly back to his paperwork.* EVERETT *approaches* ZENOBIO.*)*

ZENOBIO: Good evening, Mr Maxwell.

EVERETT: Good evening, Zeno.

ZENOBIO: How may I help you?

EVERETT: I'd like admission. To the plunge.

ZENOBIO: Any treatments? A cabinet vapor bath, a purge?

EVERETT: Just…the plunge.

ZENOBIO: Very well, that will be twenty-five—

EVERETT: Zeno, I'm sorry.

ZENOBIO: Mr Maxwell, I'm working—

EVERETT: I don't expect you to speak to me except in the minimum professional capacity, but—

ZENOBIO: Come in.

EVERETT: What?

ZENOBIO: Come in, now! We can talk, but not in the foyer.

EVERETT: You're letting me in?

ZENOBIO: Yes, but hurry. I have something to show you.

EVERETT: What about my friends?

ZENOBIO: They can't come in.

EVERETT: They have—

ZENOBIO: No one can come in. We're closed.

EVERETT: What?

ZENOBIO: We're closed, right now. Except to you. Come in quickly.

(EVERETT *glances back at* BAYARD *and* HISAYE *quizzically, then disappears into the baths.*)

ZENOBIO: We're closed!

BAYARD: But what about—?

HISAYE: You let him in without—!

BAYARD: We have our health certificates.

ZENOBIO: What?

HISAYE: *(Producing certificate)* Our certificates from the County Health Department.

BAYARD: *(Producing certificate)* We're polio-free.

HISAYE: If you let Mr Maxwell in without a certificate, surely you must let us in if we have them.

ZENOBIO: *(After a moment)* Bimini Baths is closed. You can sit here forever if you want, but right now we're closed!

*(ZENOBIO slams closed a window or places a CLOSED sign then disappears after EVERETT. Lights out on BAYARD and HISAYE and up on EVERETT and ZENOBIO inside Bimini Baths.)*

ZENOBIO: Speak quickly. I can get away with staying closed for five minutes. Any longer and I'm kaput.

EVERETT: Let them in, Zeno. It's not right. They—and you—have every right to the waters of Bimini ever day of the year.

ZENOBIO: It's my job—

EVERETT: I am a dirty—indecent person—but I appeal to your sense of decency—

ZENOBIO: That's all you wanted to tell me?

EVERETT: No. *(Pause)* You know I went to prison.

ZENOBIO: For a year.

EVERETT: I was released from San Quentin in 1918, but remained imprisoned all my life.

ZENOBIO: I'm sorry. That must be terrible.

EVERETT: For you, too.

ZENOBIO: What do you mean?

EVERETT: I'm sure you're—affected—you're what?—forty four years old, unmarried—that's my fault, I think.

ZENOBIO: What could you do worse than a war? Dachau? The world is bigger than you, worse than you! My life didn't stop with you!

EVERETT: I tied you up.

ZENOBIO: As punishment.

EVERETT: Punishment, for what?

ZENOBIO: For stealing the dire wolf baculum.

EVERETT: I don't remember—

ZENOBIO: The bone went missing, you accused me—

EVERETT: *(In tears)* No, I wrote it all down in my confession, in a notebook. I tied your hands. There was…blood—

ZENOBIO: I don't remember any blood.

EVERETT: I wrote it down!

ZENOBIO: No. No, there wasn't any blood. Writing doesn't make it true. I'll tell you what I remember.

EVERETT: What?

ZENOBIO: I asked if you loved me. And you didn't answer.

EVERETT: I do love you, Zeno.

ZENOBIO: I don't.

EVERETT: No, how could you? What I did was wrong.

ZENOBIO: It was wrong. That…is always wrong.

EVERETT: Betraying the trust of a child.

ZENOBIO: But it isn't always bad.

EVERETT: Yes, it is. Always!

ZENOBIO: I am—I'm sure—affected as you say. But I live in a world where people starve and stab and stomp each other, where buildings burn and bodies burn, you think you're important in that world? For the last thirty-two years, I hardly thought about you at all. Saw a couple of your movies. But I was thirteen. I grew up. You stayed the same. And you love me. How funny. (*He produces the bone.*)

EVERETT: You did steal it.

ZENOBIO: For a second I thought I finally had it figured out. Math. Science. Hate. Love. Nobody figures it out.

EVERETT: But we have to try.

(HISAYE *appears isolated in light.*)

EVERETT: Remedios is silent.

ZENOBIO: That's what Si said.

EVERETT: So let her in.

(*Lighting change reveals* BAYARD *next to* HISAYE. *Silently they raise their health certificates.*)

ZENOBIO: We're open.

BAYARD: Open to us?

ZENOBIO: Apologies for the delay. Bimini Baths is now open.

HISAYE: You're letting us in?

ZENOBIO: (*After a moment*) Let's see those health certificates.

EVERETT: Medium shot: Remedios accepts the certificates and lets them in. After Rustin and Yamamoto enter the baths, Remedios is confronted by Warrick and Yasunari.

(HISAYE *becomes* WARRICK *and* BAYARD *becomes* YASUNARI.)

HISAYE AS WARRICK: Zeno, have you lost your mind?

BAYARD AS YASUNARI: You're making trouble for everybody!

ZENOBIO: They have health certificates. I had to accept them.

HISAYE AS WARRICK: Not without checking with me first!

BAYARD AS YASUNARI: Listen to the boss man!

ZENOBIO: We had to let them in sooner or later.

BAYARD AS YASUNARI: That's not for you to decide.

ZENOBIO: I didn't decide it. The world changed! We had a war!

HISAYE AS WARRICK: And thank you for serving, but—

ZENOBIO: Concentration camps—in Germany—and Arizona—

BAYARD AS YASUNARI: Not the same!

ZENOBIO: I came back and everything is different!

HISAYE AS WARRICK: I'm sympathetic, but we can't change that fast.

BAYARD AS YASUNARI: We ain't Nazis!

ZENOBIO: Sometimes you just have to jump!

HISAYE AS WARRICK: Zeno, I'm sorry, but we gotta let you go.

ZENOBIO: What?

BAYARD AS YASUNARI: You're fired!

HISAYE AS WARRICK: Please go quietly and we'll call the police to take care of these Communists.

ZENOBIO: I have to—get my kit—

HISAYE AS WARRICK: We'll send your things.

ZENOBIO: But—

BAYARD AS YASUNARI: He said please.

ZENOBIO: Nope.

HISAYE AS WARRICK: What do you mean, nope?

ZENOBIO: I want that dip you promised me right now. *(He starts stripping.)*

BAYARD AS YASUNARI: What are you doing?

HISAYE AS WARRICK: Get him out.

ZENOBIO: I can even pay for it.

EVERETT: Yasunari advances on Remedios.

BAYARD AS YASUNARI: Let's go, bean-eater.

EVERETT: As he strips, Remedios reaches into his pocket.

ZENOBIO: Two Roosevelts and a Jefferson!

*(BAYARD AS YASUNARI lunges for ZENOBIO, who throws the coins at HISAYE AS WARRICK.)*

HISAYE AS WARRICK: Throw him out!

BAYARD AS YASUNARI: Fucking wetback!

*(EVERETT jumps into the fray.)*

EVERETT: Release him!

ZENOBIO: Let go of me, asshole!

HISAYE AS WARRICK: *(Restraining EVERETT)* Stay out of this, grandpa!

*(BAYARD AS YASUNARI wrestles with ZENOBIO.)*

HISAYE AS WARRICK: You're gonna get hurt!

BAYARD AS YASUNARI: I'll drown you like a kitten!

EVERETT: This is indefensible!

ZENOBIO: I paid! Let me in the pool!

HISAYE AS WARRICK: I can fire my own employees, you old cocksucker!

ZENOBIO: Let me in! Let me in!

(BAYARD AS YASUNARI *shoves* ZENOBIO, *who falls down backward. Sounds of breaking glass*)

EVERETT: Yasunari throws Remedios through a plate-glass window.

BAYARD AS YASUNARI: Are you narrating?

HISAYE AS WARRICK: My window! Goddammit, Yasunari!

EVERETT: He's bleeding!

HISAYE AS WARRICK: Get the police now! No respect for property! Communists!

(BAYARD AS YASUNARI *leaves.* EVERETT *goes to* ZENOBIO *lying there.*)

EVERETT: Zeno, you're cut!

HISAYE AS WARRICK: The police'll be here in a minute to arrest you nancies. (*Leaves*)

EVERETT: (*Helping* ZENOBIO *up*) Do you know a back way out?

ZENOBIO: I'm not leaving.

EVERETT: The police—!

ZENOBIO: I'm not leaving— (*Finishes stripping*) I'm gonna get in that plunge with all those white people and if they don't like my blood, they can get out!

(BAYARD *rushes in.*)

BAYARD: What was that crash?

EVERETT: You have to stop him!

ZENOBIO: They threw me through a window!

EVERETT: He's going to jump in the pool!

(HISAYE *runs in.*)

HISAYE: Zeno, are you okay? Your face—! *(She dabs at the blood.)*

ZENOBIO: It's Mexican Day, Si! Now every day is Mexican Day!

EVERETT: We're breaking the law!

BAYARD & HISAYE: We're changing the law!

ZENOBIO: I have to come clean about something before I jump in.

HISAYE: What?

*(ZENOBIO kisses HISAYE. It's the best kiss so far. BAYARD picks up the guitar and plays an introduction, then sings.)*

BAYARD: *(Singing)*
At Bimini the springs are hot
And soothing to the skin

*(HISAYE strips to bathing attire.)*

BAYARD & HISAYE: *(Singing)*
The world got cleaner that day, too
When Zeno let us in

*(Humming under as all four spread out into the audience. BAYARD strips to his bathing suit.)*

HISAYE: My last *Small Talk* column for the *Los Angeles Tribune* was never published, of course. Neither was Everett's screenplay. If fact, it arrived in the mail a month after he died in 1964.

*(EVERETT sees BAYARD and ZENOBIO staring at him and reluctantly strips to his bathing suit.)*

HISAYE: I put both manuscripts in a box along with the pages from his diary that I found in my leather notebook years before. I told my children to destroy the contents upon my death. Children, however, are often disobedient. I don't mind: after all, it wasn't just my story.

EVERETT: Nor mine.

BAYARD & ZENOBIO: Nor mine.

HISAYE: *(To an audience member)* It's your story.

BAYARD & EVERETT: *(To an audience member)* And yours.

HISAYE: *(To an audience member)* You're in it.

EVERETT: *(To an audience member)* You, too.

BAYARD: The story isn't over.

HISAYE: We're in the middle of it.

ZENOBIO: All of us together.

HISAYE: As was the case for most public bathing facilities in those days, the reluctant welcome of Bimini Baths wore out just a few years later.

ALL:
At Bimini the spring was capped
In nineteen fifty-one
The baths were closed forever then
To us and everyone

*(Sound of a police siren. They all dash back onto the stage.)*

EVERETT: I told you! Here they come!

BAYARD: Let's make them work for it!

HISAYE: *(Takes ZENOBIO'S hand)* Quick!

BAYARD: Ready?

ZENOBIO: Jump!

BAYARD: Jump!

BAYARD, HISAYE, ZENNOBIO: Jump!

EVERETT: Fade to black.

*(They all jump. A big splash)*

END OF PLAY

www.ingramcontent.com/pod-product-compliance
Lightning Source LLC
Chambersburg PA
CBHW052211090426
42741CB00010B/2497